TAXI OF TERROR

'Good luck Jack. Don't forget us!' Jack's work friends are saying goodbye to him. They are having a party for him because he is leaving for a new job. He gets a card and a present – a mobile phone. Jack's friends are sad, but the party is good and they all dance for hours.

Then Jack leaves the party. He's tired and he wants to go home. 'It's cold,' he thinks. He looks for a taxi, but he can't find one. He walks for a long time – he is getting very tired. Then, at last, he sees a taxi. Great! Now he can go home and sleep!

But this is only the beginning of a long night – a long night in the taxi of terror!

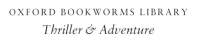

OXFORD BOOKWORMS LIBRARY
Thriller & Adventure

Taxi of Terror

Starter (250 headwords)

PHILLIP BURROWS AND MARK FOSTER

Taxi of Terror

OXFORD UNIVERSITY PRESS

OXFORD

UNIVERSITY PRESS

Great Clarendon Street, Oxford OX2 6DP

Oxford University Press is a department of the University of Oxford.
It furthers the University's objective of excellence in research, scholarship,
and education by publishing worldwide in

Oxford New York

Auckland Cape Town Dar es Salaam Hong Kong Karachi
Kuala Lumpur Madrid Melbourne Mexico City Nairobi
New Delhi Shanghai Taipei Toronto

With offices in

Argentina Austria Brazil Chile Czech Republic France Greece
Guatemala Hungary Italy Japan Poland Portugal Singapore
South Korea Switzerland Thailand Turkey Ukraine Vietnam

OXFORD and OXFORD ENGLISH are registered trade marks of
Oxford University Press in the UK and in certain other countries

ISBN: 978 0 19 423418 4

Printed in Hong Kong

Word count (main text): 970

For more information on the Oxford Bookworms Library, visit
www.oup.com/bookworms

CONTENTS

STORY INTRODUCTION   i

Taxi of Terror   1

GLOSSARY   25

ACTIVITIES: Before Reading   29

ACTIVITIES: While Reading   30

ACTIVITIES: After Reading   32

ABOUT THE AUTHORS   34

ABOUT THE BOOKWORMS LIBRARY   35

TAXI OF TERROR

Everybody is having a good time.

Good-bye, everyone. Thank you, again, for my present.

See you soon.

Take care.

Enjoy yourself.

It's cold. Where's a taxi?

It's late – but I don't have to work tomorrow. Now, how do I get home?

Jack cannot find a taxi. He walks for a long time and gets very tired.

At last, Jack sees a taxi.

I live at 57 Park Road. Can you take me there?

Of course. Get in. You look tired.

Yes, I'm very tired.

It's very quiet tonight, sir. You're only my second passenger . . . Sir?

It's late. He needs his bed.

The taxi stops at a traffic light. Suddenly . . .

What the . . .

Say nothing.

Do what I tell you . . . or you're dead.

He has a gun! I don't understand. Am I dreaming?

At the roundabout turn right.

The taxi driver drives very carefully now.

OK. I must keep calm. Everything's OK. He can't see me here.

Don't do that. I don't like surprises.

Now, get out of the taxi. Slowly.

Driver, open the boot of the taxi.

What?

Just do it!

How can we get home? Look there's a taxi.

I've got a gun. You haven't! Do you want me to shoot?

No. Please. Don't shoot.

Now, I want the police.
9 . . .
9 . . .
9 . . .

Beep!

Hello. Police.

Yes! it works. We're all right now.

Jack phones the police station and talks to a policewoman.

Can I help you?

A man's in our taxi. He's got a gun. I don't know where he wants to go. He's very dangerous.

OK,
keep calm.
What's your
name
and where
are you?

I'm Jack and I'm in the boot of the taxi.

OK, Jack.
Tell me about
the man.

He's little and thin, and he has a bad eye and red hair. He has a little beard.

You know who that is?
It's the Wolf.

Jack, that man's very dangerous. He's called the Wolf and we're looking for him. Be careful. We must find where you are. Can you see anything?

It's about five minutes to the airport. We must stop the Wolf.

Drive to the airport. I must get on that plane.

The Wolf races into the airport.

The car isn't moving now. I can hear planes. I think we're at the airport!

Later the police bring the Wolf back into the airport building.

GLOSSARY

banana something you eat; it grows on trees
calm not angry
clever you are clever if you understand things easily
dangerous something that can hurt you is dangerous
enjoy like doing something
great very good
hurt be in pain; a broken leg hurts
job work people do to earn money
kind if you are good to other people you are kind
loud a noise that is not quiet
luck you have luck if good things happen to you
ouch what you say when you are in pain
seagull a bird that lives by the sea
tunnel where a road goes under the ground
turn change the way you are going
way a road or course
wolf a wild animal; it is like a big dog

Taxi of Terror

ACTIVITIES

ACTIVITIES

Before Reading

1 Look at the front and back cover of the book. Now complete these sentences.

1 The taxi in the story is . . .

   a ☐ black.

   b ☐ yellow.

   c ☐ blue.

2 Imagine you are the taxi driver. You are . . .

   a ☐ afraid.

   b ☐ happy.

   c ☐ not interested.

3 The story happens. . .

   a ☐ in a town.

   b ☐ in the country.

   c ☐ not in a or b.

4 At the end of the story the police catch . . .

   a ☐ a bad man.

   b ☐ the taxi driver.

   c ☐ Jack.

ACTIVITIES

While Reading

1 Read pages 1–6, then answer these questions.

1 Why is Jack leaving his job?
2 How does Jack decide to get home?
3 Where does the taxi stop?

2 Read pages 7–12, then answer these questions.

1 Does the Wolf want money?
2 Does the taxi turn right or left next to the hospital?
3 Write a description of the Wolf.

....

....

....

4 What is the number of the Taxi?

3 Read pages 13–18.
Are these sentences true (T) or false (F)?

	T	F
1 He gets in the boot of the taxi .	☐	☐
2 He phones his mum.	☐	☐
3 He escapes from the boot.	☐	☐
4 He talks to a policeman.	☐	☐
5 He tells the police the Wolf has a small nose.	☐	☐
6 He hears a clock.	☐	☐

4 Read pages 19–24. Complete the sentences with the following words:

airport beard boot plane seagulls

1

Now I can hear lots of ..... Are we near the sea?

2

Drive to the ..... I must get on that .....

3

Are you looking for that bad man with the ..... ? He's over there.

4

Can someone open the ..... ?

ACTIVITIES

After Reading

1 **Answer these questions.**

1 Who

a . . . does the Wolf put in the boot of the taxi?

b . . . does Jack call on his mobile phone?

c . . . gets knocked over by the Wolf?

d . . . says: 'That's £16.50 please'?

2 What

a . . . almost crashes into the taxi?

b . . . is the Wolf trying to catch?

c . . . can Jack hear at the dump?

d . . . do the police look at on the wall?

3 Where

a . . . does the taxi go over some bumps?

b . . . is Jack at the beginning of the story?

c . . . do the police catch up with the Wolf?

d . . . does the Wolf get in the taxi?

2 **Put these sentences in the correct order.**

a ☐ The taxi drives next to a rubbish dump.

b ☐ The taxi arrives at the airport.

c ☐ Jack calls the police with his mobile phone.

d ☐ The taxi drives through a tunnel.

e ☐ The taxi drives near a clock.

3 **Use these words to fill in the gaps.**

airport boot catch gun hear job
mobile phone pleased police taxi

Jack is leaving his old .... His friends give him a ....
as a leaving present. He is very .... On his way home
Jack falls asleep in a .... Suddenly at some traffic lights,
a dangerous man called the Wolf gets in the taxi – he has a
.... The taxi driver does what the Wolf tells him. Jack
wakes up and is soon put in the ....of the taxi. Then he
has an idea – he calls the .... with his phone. Jack tells
them what he can .... from inside the boot. The police
find out that the taxi is driving to the .... The police get
there just in time to .... the Wolf.

ABOUT THE AUTHORS

Mark Foster and Phillip Burrows have worked as a writer/illustrator team since 1991. They were born three years and many miles apart, but they are very nearly twins. They drive the same car, work on the same computers, and wear the same wellington boots – but not at the same time! They spend all the money they get from writing on gadgets, but please don't tell their wives. Mark and Phill have worked together on several Bookworms titles, including *Starman* (Starter, Fantasy & Horror) and *Escape* (Starter, Thriller & Adventure). When they meet to write, they like to go to expensive hotels, eat chips dipped in coffee, and laugh at their own jokes.

OXFORD BOOKWORMS LIBRARY

Classics • Crime & Mystery • Factfiles • Fantasy & Horror
Human Interest • Playscripts • Thriller & Adventure
True Stories • World Stories

The OXFORD BOOKWORMS LIBRARY provides enjoyable reading in English, with a wide range of classic and modern fiction, non-fiction, and plays. It includes original and adapted texts in seven carefully graded language stages, which take learners from beginner to advanced level. An overview is given on the next pages.

All Stage 1 titles are available as audio recordings, as well as over eighty other titles from Starter to Stage 6. All Starters and many titles at Stages 1 to 4 are specially recommended for younger learners. Every Bookworm is illustrated, and Starters and Factfiles have full-colour illustrations.

The OXFORD BOOKWORMS LIBRARY also offers extensive support. Each book contains an introduction to the story, notes about the author, a glossary, and activities. Additional resources include tests and worksheets, and answers for these and for the activities in the books. There is advice on running a class library, using audio recordings, and the many ways of using Oxford Bookworms in reading programmes. Resource materials are available on the website <www.oup.com/bookworms>.

The *Oxford Bookworms Collection* is a series for advanced learners. It consists of volumes of short stories by well-known authors, both classic and modern. Texts are not abridged or adapted in any way, but carefully selected to be accessible to the advanced student.

You can find details and a full list of titles in the *Oxford Bookworms Library Catalogue* and *Oxford English Language Teaching Catalogues*, and on the website <www.oup.com/bookworms>.

THE OXFORD BOOKWORMS LIBRARY
GRADING AND SAMPLE EXTRACTS

STARTER • 250 HEADWORDS

present simple – present continuous – imperative –
can/cannot, must – *going to* (future) – simple gerunds …

Her phone is ringing – but where is it?

Sally gets out of bed and looks in her bag. No phone. She looks under the bed. No phone. Then she looks behind the door. There is her phone. Sally picks up her phone and answers it. *Sally's Phone*

STAGE 1 • 400 HEADWORDS

… past simple – coordination with *and*, *but*, *or* –
subordination with *before*, *after*, *when*, *because*, *so* …

I knew him in Persia. He was a famous builder and I worked with him there. For a time I was his friend, but not for long. When he came to Paris, I came after him – I wanted to watch him. He was a very clever, very dangerous man. *The Phantom of the Opera*

STAGE 2 • 700 HEADWORDS

… present perfect – *will* (future) – *(don't) have to, must not, could* –
comparison of adjectives – simple *if* clauses – past continuous –
tag questions – *ask/tell* + infinitive …

While I was writing these words in my diary, I decided what to do. I must try to escape. I shall try to get down the wall outside. The window is high above the ground, but I have to try. I shall take some of the gold with me – if I escape, perhaps it will be helpful later. *Dracula*

STAGE 3 • 1000 HEADWORDS

... should, may – present perfect continuous – *used to* – past perfect –
causative – relative clauses – indirect statements ...

Of course, it was most important that no one should see Colin, Mary, or Dickon entering the secret garden. So Colin gave orders to the gardeners that they must all keep away from that part of the garden in future. *The Secret Garden*

STAGE 4 • 1400 HEADWORDS

... past perfect continuous – passive (simple forms) –
would conditional clauses – indirect questions –
relatives with *where/when* – gerunds after prepositions/phrases ...

I was glad. Now Hyde could not show his face to the world again. If he did, every honest man in London would be proud to report him to the police. *Dr Jekyll and Mr Hyde*

STAGE 5 • 1800 HEADWORDS

... future continuous – future perfect –
passive (modals, continuous forms) –
would have conditional clauses – modals + perfect infinitive ...

If he had spoken Estella's name, I would have hit him. I was so angry with him, and so depressed about my future, that I could not eat the breakfast. Instead I went straight to the old house. *Great Expectations*

STAGE 6 • 2500 HEADWORDS

... passive (infinitives, gerunds) – advanced modal meanings –
clauses of concession, condition

When I stepped up to the piano, I was confident. It was as if I knew that the prodigy side of me really did exist. And when I started to play, I was so caught up in how lovely I looked that I didn't worry how I would sound. *The Joy Luck Club*

BOOKWORMS · THRILLER & ADVENTURE · STARTER

Escape

PHILLIP BURROWS AND MARK FOSTER

'I'm not a thief. I'm an innocent man,' shouts Brown. He is angry because he is in prison and the prison guards hate him. Then one day Brown has an idea. It is dangerous – very dangerous.

BOOKWORMS · THRILLER & ADVENTURE · STARTER

Orca

PHILLIP BURROWS AND MARK FOSTER

When Tonya and her friends decide to sail around the world they want to see exciting things and visit exciting places.

But one day, they meet an orca – a killer whale – one of the most dangerous animals in the sea. And life gets a little too exciting.

BOOKWORMS · CRIME & MYSTERY · STARTER

Give us the Money

MAEVE CLARKE

'Every day is the same. Nothing exciting ever happens to me,' thinks Adam one boring Monday morning. But today is not the same. When he helps a beautiful young woman because some men want to take her bag, life gets exciting and very, very dangerous.

BOOKWORMS · FANTASY & HORROR · STARTER

Starman

PHILLIP BURROWS AND MARK FOSTER

The empty centre of Australia. The sun is hot and there are not many people. And when Bill meets a man, alone, standing on an empty road a long way from anywhere, he is surprised and worried.

And Bill is right to be worried. Because there is something strange about the man he meets. Very strange . . .

BOOKWORMS · THRILLER & ADVENTURE · STAGE 1

The President's Murderer

JENNIFER BASSETT

The President is dead!

A man is running in the night. He is afraid and needs to rest. But there are people behind him – people with lights, and dogs, and guns.

A man is standing in front of a desk. His boss is very angry, and the man is tired and needs to sleep. But first he must find the other man, and bring him back – dead or alive.

Two men: the hunter and the hunted. Which will win and which will lose?

Long live the President!

BOOKWORMS · THRILLER & ADVENTURE · STAGE 1

White Death

TIM VICARY

Sarah Harland is nineteen, and she is in prison. At the airport, they find heroin in her bag. So, now she is waiting to go to court. If the court decides that it was her heroin, then she must die.

She says she did not do it. But if she did not, who did? Only two people can help Sarah: her mother, and an old boyfriend who does not love her now. Can they work together? Can they find the real criminal before it is too late?